For Sylvia and Sophie…Kirk and Paul…Home and Love

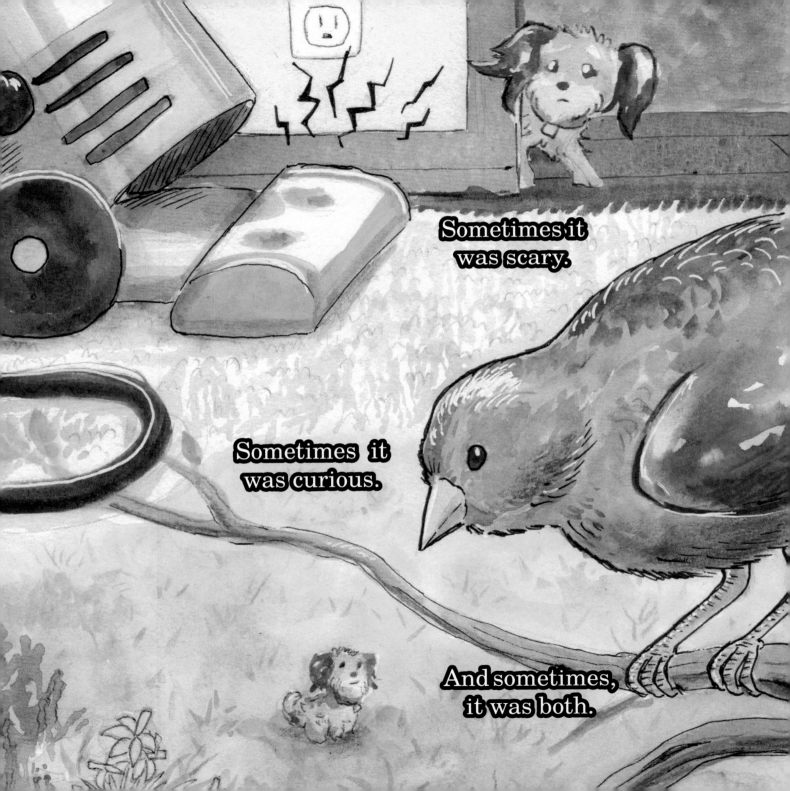

I had lots of opportunities to explore and to decide if life was a good thing...

I hated going to find them, but every time I did, they made me feel loved a lot again, so it was worth it.

Sometimes we licked each other
(or really, I licked them).
Sometimes we whispered in each others ears
(or I tried to lick inside their ears).
Sometimes we went nose to nose, tooth to tooth
and sometimes they let me sniff their toes!

In other words,
sometimes they spoke dog!

We did lots of things together. First, we lived in an old house and then we made a new house.

I didn't like that at all because nothing seemed right but people call that moving and it seems they do it a lot.

I decided that as long as I was with them I would try to be happy and eventually I was.

Each year, I had a birthday...
that meant I got bigger.
We had visits with old people
and new people, and then more
new people.

Sometimes there were scary toys and noisy mechanical things and, every now and again, without even going for a walk, there was a tree right inside our house!

When my people went away I was sad.

When my people came back I was excited and run around happy!

As I grew up I found out that
I had many different feelings,
experiences and faces...
my people loved them all!

Everyday was a little different but a lot the same.

Clothes came and went.

Toys came and (mercifully) went.

Seasons came and went.

Still, my favorite part was always when they came back with their silly clothes, annoying toys and their ideas about putting me in and on things that made them laugh.

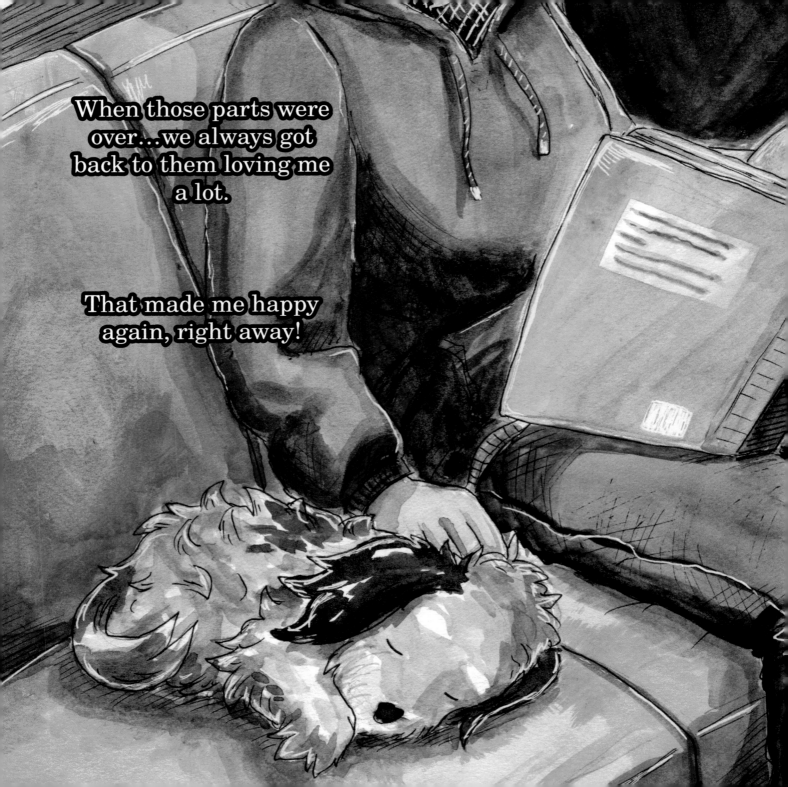

I've learned that life gives you a lot of different experiences and sometimes what it all means is a puzzle!

Still, every day I feel loved a lot by my people... whether they're right here or far away.

I smell them on our rugs and in our furniture.

I remember them rubbing my belly. I taste them on my treats and sometimes, I wait at the window for them to come back, and by some mysterious workings, they always do!

They are my Home.

That is Love.

Made in the USA
Columbia, SC
16 April 2017